WORLD'S GREATEST PUT DOWN LINES

BY

PATRICK HANIFIN
&
BUTCH FISCO

ILLUSTRATED BY

DESMOND MULLAN

CCC PUBLICATIONS • LOS ANGELES

Published by

CCC Publications
21630 Lassen Street
Chatsworth, CA 91311

Manufactured in the United States Of America

Cover © 1994 CCC Publications

Interior illustrations © 1994 CCC Publications

Cover art by Lucques

Interior art by Desmond Mullan

Cover/Interior layout & production by Oasis Graphics

ISBN: 0-918259-59-2

If your local U.S. bookstore is out of stock, copies of this book may be obtained by mailing check or money order for $4.99 per book (plus $2.50 to cover postage and handling) to: CCC Publications; 21630 Lassen St.; Chatsworth, CA 91311.

Pre-publication Edition – 8/94

Second Printing – 7/95

Third Printing - 9/95

Acknowledgements

We would like to thank, first of all, our parents, Emma and Vince Fisco, and Doris Hanifin, for their continuous support and enthusiasm during this project and especially, our valued friend, Mike Autrey.

We would also like to thank the more than 5,000 comedians who use these hilarious put down lines during their nightly shows throughout the country.

And last but not least, we would like to thank all the obnoxious hecklers, because without them we wouldn't be writing this book.

Introduction

In Las Vegas, a comedian is performing his act in a sold-out showroom. Suddenly a waitress trips and drops her tray of drinks, shattering them on the floor. Without hesitation, the comedian replies, "You can just set those drinks down anywhere!" The audience laughs loudly.

In Hollywood at the Comedy Store, a comedian on stage is suddenly interrupted during his show by a drunken man who yells out in an incoherent manner, "What do you do for a living?" Without hesitation, the comedian replies, "I find your mother dates!" The crowd roars and applauds. The comedian responds again to the heckler, "Didn't I see you earlier? Yeah, you were in the bathroom getting a drink of water, and the seat fell on your head!" The crowd applauds.

A few blocks away at the Improv Comedy Club, the comedian on stage is interrupted by an obnoxious lady with bleached blonde hair. Without hesitation, the comedian responds, "Relax Sybil. I work alone!" The crowd laughs loudly. The comic responds again, "Hey lady, I like how you dye the roots of your hair brown!" The crowd cheers.

What all these comedians have in common are the hilarious put-down lines that they use to quiet their annoying hecklers and to keep control of their show. These funny put-down lines are known as standards or stock lines in the world of stand-up comedy. They are, without a doubt, the best comedy lines in the business, and regardless of how rough a heckler is, these lines never fail.

If YOU ever have to speak before a group, these lines could save your butt. Many put-down lines that work on stage will work just as well at a party or any public gathering. By memorizing a few of these lines you can be the life of the party.

This book is broken down into two sections. The first half is called, ALL-AROUND PUT-DOWNS. These are lines anybody can use at a party, bar, restaurant, or any public place where someone is being obnoxious.

The second section contains put down lines for COMEDIANS OR PUBLIC SPEAKERS. All these lines apply to a stage situation or whenever you're in front of a group of people.

Finally, before completing our book, we couldn't resist adding a bonus section, **"Patrick and Butch's Favorite Jokes."** These are some of the best jokes ever told, and we hope you will love them!

So have fun with our collection of outrageous comedy put-downs, and if you find our book too raunchy or tasteless, all we have to say is, give it to someone you hate.

Patrick Hanifin

Butch Fisco

CONTENTS

All-Around Put-Downs

Put Down Lines for the Comedian/Public Speaker

SECTION I

* * * * *

ALL-AROUND PUT-DOWNS

ANNOYING PEOPLE

I saw this guy earlier! He was in the bathroom getting a drink of water – then the seat fell and hit him on the head!

* * * * * * *

You're such a smart ass! I bet you could sit on a carton of ice cream and tell what flavor it is!

* * * * * * *

(To friend, re: obnoxious lady)
This is the last time I ever bring my mom here!

* * * * * * *

(To someone who keeps up a constant chatter)
Excuse me, sir, but have you ever heard the expression, "Shut the F * * k up!"

* * * * * * *

Now I know why some animals eat their young!

Hey, I don't come down to where you're working
and bother you there at McDonald's, do I?

APPEARANCE

Is that your face or did your neck throw up?

* * * * * * *

(To a woman who criticizes your appearance)
Lady, there's not enough makeup in the world to
make you look good!

* * * * * * *

Nice teeth! Bet you could eat corn through
a fence with those!

* * * * * * *

Didn't I see your picture on an abortion pamphlet?

* * * * * * *

(To a woman with a lot of makeup)
Your makeup is so thick I could draw on your face
with my finger!

* * * * * * *

(To a woman who criticizes your appearance)
Yeah, and you're so ugly, your makeup mirror
needs safety glass!

CITIES/STATES

I just got back from Arkansas and it sure is nice to see people with teeth again!

* * * * * * *

Are you from the Midwest? Okay, I'll speak slower!

* * * * * * *

(To person from New York)
Let me make you feel at home!
(Make your hand into a gun)
Bang! Bang!

* * * * * * *

Where are you from?
(When no response)
Can you guess?

CLOTHES

Nice suit! Is that from your Communion?

* * * * * *

Interesting shirt! I passed that one up
when I was in K-Mart!

* * * * * *

(To a man wearing a cowbow hat)
Is that your Tractor parked in the lot?

* * * * * *

Nice dress! Is that from your prom?

* * * * * *

Nice suit! Somewhere there's a Pinto
without upholstery!

COUPLES & DATES

(Re: A young, good-looking couple)
Great! We have Barbie and Ken here tonight!

* * * * * * *

(Re: Two guys and a girl)
What happened? Computer date screw-up?

* * * * * * *

Are you two dating? Married? Oh, this is a
business trip!

* * * * * * *

(Re: Any unmarried couple)
So, what're you two – a Love Connection date?

* * * * * * *

This is why second cousins should not marry!

COUPLES & DATES

(Re: Young couple)
I didn't know the prom was tonight!

* * * * * * *

(To an overly affectionate couple)
Why don't you just go check into a Motel!

* * * * * * *

(Re: Young couple)
First date? Why don't you give her a kiss to break the ice?
Okay, great! Now try for some titty!

* * * * * * *

So, are you guys dating...or just using each other?

* * * * * * *

(To an overly affectionate couple)
You mind getting your hand out of his crotch,
you're making me horny!

Is that your date or are you a social worker?

DRUGS

(Re: Loud person who slurs their words)
What happened, did the Quaaludes just kick in?

* * * * * * *

You're obviously wasted! Did you bring enough drugs
for everyone?

* * * * * * *

(When a person is obviously not making any sense)
You know, you have the I.Q. of a carrot!

* * * * * * *

(Re: Incoherent remark)
Let me look that up in my Quaalude dictionary!

DRUNKS

(When a drunk blurts out something stupid)
Whatever drugs you're on, will you give us some?

* * * * * * *

Yeah, I remember my first beer!

* * * * * * *

Please, have another drink and pass out!

* * * * * * *

*(A smart-mouthed drunk asks you what
you do for a living)*
I get dates for your mom!

GROUP OF WOMEN

Nice to see you girls are off the streets for a change!

* * * * * * *

What is this...a Mary Kay party?

* * * * * * *

Bachelorette party ladies...or lesbians night out?

* * * * * * *

What happened, the strip club closed tonight?

* * * * * * *

(Male - in response to rude remark)
Hey ladies, at least when I take a piss, I can write my name in the snow!

* * * * * * *

(To two women hassling you)
This is cool, stereo bimbos!

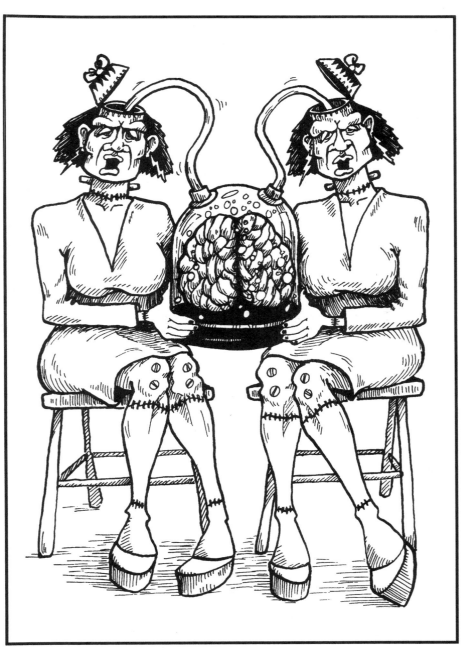

(When two women hassle you)
What is this, two people sharing a brain?

HAIR

Nice hair! What is that, rayon?

* * * * * * *

(Lady with a big hairdo)
Hey lady, something just flew out of your hair!

* * * * * * *

(To a bleached blonde)
Interesting, I see you dye your roots brown!

* * * * * * *

(Lady with a big hairdo)
Is that really your hair or a nest?

INTERRUPTIONS

I bet when you're at home you talk back to the TV!

* * * * * *

(Re: Ongoing chatter)
Hey lady, put the vibrator on low!

* * * * * *

Hey lady, leave me alone! I don't come down to where you're working and jump on the bed, do I?

* * * * * *

(When something falls while you're speaking, acknowledge it...)
Once again, gravity rears its ugly head!

* * * * * *

(When a siren is heard from outside)
Well, I've got to go, my ride's here!

LATE ARRIVERS
(Can be used at parties)

It's amateur strip night and your next!

* * * * * * *

The babysitter called and said not to worry...
it's only a head wound!

* * * * * * *

We all just finished standing up and telling a little bit
about ourselves! Now it's your turn!

* * * * * * *

Do you people have a note from your parents?

* * * * * * *

What happened...the bowling league got canceled tonight?

LATE ARRIVERS

What happened...did the Amway meeting last longer
than you expected?

* * * * * * *

Could I get you something...like maybe a watch?

* * * * * * *

(To embarrass a man)
The Elks Club is next door, sir!

* * * * * * *

(To embarrass a woman)
Took you longer than usual to hitchhike, huh?

LOUD MOUTHS

If your dick was half as big as your mouth,
you would have a date!

* * * * * * *

(When a woman laughs in an annoying tone)
Can we get some oil over here?

* * * * * * *

(To someone with annoying laugh)
Nice laugh! You ever think about working in
a haunted house?

* * * * * * *

Do you know sign language?
(Flip person off)

Guys like you make women become lesbians!

MEN

(To a "stuffy" guy)
I'll bet you're the kind of guy who gets out
of the shower to take a pee!

* * * * * * *

You're the kind of guy who gets all of his knowledge from
the National Enquirer

* * * * * * *

What's the matter? K-Mart lay you off today

* * * * * * *

I'd call you a C * * k sucker, but I know
you're trying to quit!

* * * * * * *

Did your mom have any kids that lived?

* * * * * * *

Over eighty million sperm and yours had to make it!

PARTY PICKER-UPPERS

I read in the newspaper where one-third of the people in the world are ugly! Now I want everyone to look at the person on your left! Now everyone look at the person on your right! If those people look okay, then YOU'RE it!

* * * * * * *

Does anyone here have a cigarette? How about a light? How about some cash and jewelry?

* * * * * * *

By a show of hands, how many people have never been here before? And how many people are here for the first time?
(Note: Both questions are the same)

* * * * * * *

Hey, is everyone having a fun time? Great, because my cousins are out robbing your cars!

* * * * * * *

(Tell everyone)
The next time someone comes in let's all point at him or her and laugh real loud!

RESTROOMS

(Note: Can be used in restaurants, bars or at parties)

(When someone is gone a very short time)
Boy, that was really quick! What did you do spit?

* * * * * * *

(When a woman gets up to leave, cup your hands around your mouth and make an announcement)
All lesbians to the restroom!

* * * * * * *

(When two guys go to the restroom together, pretend to be one of them talking)
"Come on. I'll show you my dick!"

* * * * * * *

(When someone returns from the restroom)
Did you wash your hands?

* * * * * * *

(Re: someone seen going to the restroom a second time)
Make sure to keep it in the toilet bowl this time!

(To someone returning from the restroom)
Hey, nice stains!

RESTROOMS

(When a man gets up to leave, cup your hands around your mouth and make an announcement)
All homosexuals to the restroom!

* * * * * * *

(As a guy heads for the restroom)
Don't forget to shake it good so it doesn't drip!

* * * * * * *

(As someone gets up to go to the restroom)
You need an extra straw or razor blade?

* * * * * * *

(Girls always seem to go to the restroom in pairs. When two girls go together, pretend to be one of them talking...)
"Come on, girlfriend! Let's go shopping!"

SEXUAL INNUENDOES

(To a guy)
Do you know what a well satisfied woman says?
No...I didn't think so!

* * * * * * *

I'll bet a big night for you is getting drunk
and petting farm animals!

* * * * * * *

Remember your best sex?
That yelling, screaming, going wild type of thing?
In your case, I'm sure you were alone!

* * * * * * *

Hey lady, just curious, is there anyone here you have not
slept with?

* * * * * * *

Lady, you've been poked so many times you
look like a pin cushion!

SEXUAL INNUENDOES

(To tease a guy when he's with his girlfriend)
Wow! This guy's been here every night with
a different date!

* * * * * * *

(Man to woman)
Do you have any Italian in you?
No...would you like some?

* * * * * * *

(Man to woman)
I'd rather cut it off than give it to you!

* * * * * * *

After meeting you, I now believe in birth control!

* * * * * * *

I have a joke that will knock your boobs off...
oh, I see you have already heard it!

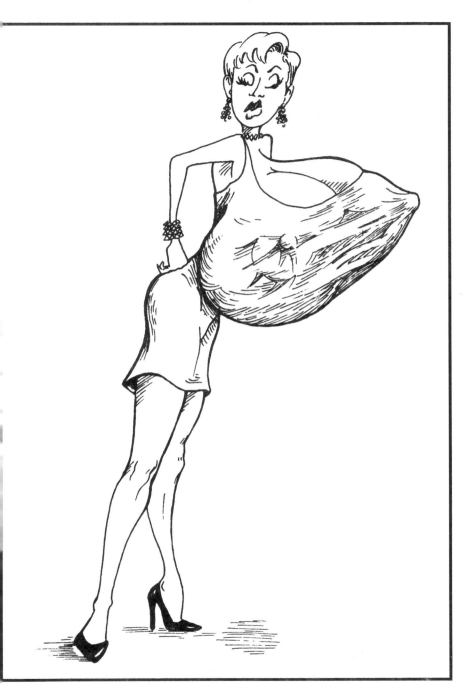

(To a woman obviously proud of her cleavage)
Nice boobs! Bet those cost some money!

TOTALLY OBNOXIOUS PEOPLE

Why don't you put a condom over your head? If you're going to act like a dick, you might as well look like one!

* * * * * * *

If I want to hear from an A* * hole, I'll fart!

* * * * * * *

Why is it the guys with the smallest dicks have the biggest mouths?

* * * * * * *

Why don't you go roll your face in some dough and make A* * hole cookies!

* * * * * * *

Now I know what happens when the fetus doesn't get enough oxygen!

* * * * * * *

(When a man is sitting with his arms folded across his chest)
What's the matter, Sir, your nipples hard?
(Or: At your own risk, also may be used for a woman)

* * * * * * *

I'm very disappointed! I was just going to do my impression of an A * * hole and this guy beat me to it!

WAITRESSES

Please tip the waitress! She has three kids and
one of them is mine!

* * * * * * *

Waitress, bring this lady a drink...and charge it
to the guy over there!

* * * * * * *

(Waitress drops her tray)
Just set that anywhere!

* * * * * * *

Please tip the waitresses! They need the money
for makeup!

* * * * * * *

(Waitress drops her tray)
Next time we will use safety nets!

* * * * * * *

Please tip the waitresses! They're all hookers and it
will keep them off the streets!

Please tip the waitress! She needs the money to get back to the clinic!

WOMEN
(EXTREMELY OBNOXIOUS)

(To a lady who keeps yelling)
Hey, relax Sybil!

* * * * * * *

Lady, there's not enough alcohol in the world for
me to sleep with you!

* * * * * * *

I can't think of anything worse than waking up at 7 AM,
rolling over and seeing you next to me!

* * * * * * *

What do you and a Tampax have in common?
Both are stuck up bitches!

* * * * * * *

Women like you make guys become gay!

SECTION II

* * * * *

PUT-DOWNS
FOR
COMEDIANS
& PUBLIC
SPEAKERS

BAD SHOW

What...did you guys all get together before the show and decide to come here and ruin my career?

* * * * * * *

(When you get to the end of a show that's gone badly and have gotten little response, make fun of yourself by pretending you're doing great)
I've got to go now!
(No response)
Okay, I'll stay!

* * * * * * *

What is this? An audience or an oil painting?

* * * * * * *

(When the show's obviously too long)
Don't anyone try to leave! The doors are locked and we are going to be here until 5:00 A.M.!

* * * * * * *

(Little or no crowd response)
How many English speaking people do we have here tonight?

BAD SHOW

(When people are reluctant to laugh)
Folks, make sure you laugh! If you hold it in you will fart!

* * * * * * *

(When you're doing a joke about someone famous and an audience member is offended)
Like you know *(name person)* personally and are going to call them up and tell them!

* * * * * * *

(When your time is up)
Well, I've got to go! My hooker's ready!

* * * * * * *

By the way, my real job is to clear this room!

CROWDS - GENERAL

(For a dead crowd)
Is this your first time together as an audience?

* * * * * * *

There's good crowds and there's bad crowds, and I just
want to say, you've been a crowd!

* * * * * * *

(When a crowd gets rowdy, make fun of yourself)
At what point did I lose control?

* * * * * * *

(For a rowdy crowd)
Wha-da-ya-say, Let's just forget about the speech and beat
the crap out of each other!

* * * * * * *

How you doing, folks?
*(If no response from the audience, point out the
obvious for a laugh)*
You look pissed!

CROWDS - GENERAL

(When different members are incoherent)
Why don't you guys put your words together and
make a whole sentence?

* * * * * * *

(Re: Small crowd)
This looks like a bad New Years Eve party?

* * * * * * *

(To a group of women)
You girls looking for some guys later? Say, yes,
or we will think you're all lesbians!

* * * * * * *

(Re: Small crowd)
Did you all come together in a bus?

* * * * * * *

You're from Iraq! *(or other foreign country of ill-repute)*
No, that's okay! Be proud! This is America!
We're all free! In fact, stand up and take a bow!
Okay everyone...take aim and...FIRE!

What happened? Did you all ride together and your truck broke down and you said, "Hey look, comedy *(or what ever the event is).* **Let's go in there!"**

DRIVING

Please drive home carefully! I heard that a person gets hit every 15 seconds – and he's really getting pissed off!

* * * * * * *

Anyone here drive a brown '72 Pinto, license number 2EDL497? We would like to ask you to please move it! It's legally parked, but it's a piece of crap and it is embarrassing this establishment!

* * * * * * *

Remember as you leave that a lot of people have been drinking tonight and there's a lot of dangerous people on the road, so drive home as fast as you can!

* * * * * * *

(Men always abandon their male friends
when they meet a woman...)
Who's driving? You know if he scores tonight, you guys are hitchhiking home!

* * * * * * *

(When you mention a State and someone applauds)
Oh great, can I have a ride home?

GROUP OF MEN

(Say in a spirit of fun)
You guys going to look for women tonight? Say yes, or
we will think you're all gay!

* * * * * * *

(To make fun of men without dates)
Bachelor party...or fags' night out?

* * * * * * *

Can't you see these guys driving around in a van,
drinking beer, looking at the nude women in National
Geographic Magazine, saying, "It doesn't get
any better than this!"

* * * * * * *

(Mock exasperation)
Great, guy groupies! Just what I need...these guys follow
me all over the country!

* * * * * * *

(To imply a group of dressed-up men are all nerds)
Check it out – They're all wearing clip-on ties!

INTERRUPTIONS

Keep it up! I just want to remind you I can piss
on you from here!

* * * * * * *

(When people in the crowd say things back and forth)
Great! Now the audience is heckling themselves!

* * * * * * *

(When someone blurts out loudly)
Thanks for bringing my speech *(act)* to a complete halt!

* * * * * * *

(The crowd is laughing to themselves)
You people don't need me, do you, you could just
entertain yourselves!

* * * * * * *

(A drunk mumbles loudly)
Just yell out any incoherent thing!

* * * * * * *

*(When you're speaking to someone and another person
yells out across the room)*
And you're a ventriloquist, too!

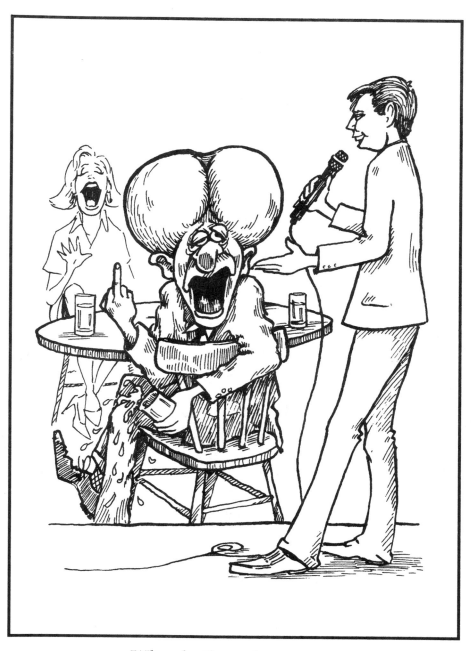

**Why do they always put
the biggest A* * holes up front?**

INTERRUPTIONS

(When there's more than one heckler, dangle the microphone from the cord into the audience)
Let's go fishing for A * * holes!

* * * * * * *

Excuse me, was I talking while you were?

* * * * * * *

Hey relax, I work alone!

* * * * * * *

Look, two people just walked in!
Now I have to start over!
(Then quickly redo the highlights of your entire act)

* * * * * * *

(When a man continually heckles you)
This is the retarded son of the owner!

M C

(Long show)
You guys are in luck! Thirty-seven more speakers/comics
just walked in the door!

* * * * * * *

(When there's a lot of smoke on stage)
Could I get a little more smoke up here, please! I want to
die from lung cancer tonight!

* * * * * * *

What's your name?
(When a man responds, "John")
What do you know, there's a room in the back
named after you

* * * * * * *

Anyone here a lawyer *(or other questionable occupation)*?
No...good! Then let's talk about them weasels!

M C

(When you're talking about sex and a guy yells out)
Thank you for your comment, sir!
The guy back there in a raincoat!

* * * * * * *

(To introduce a comedian or the next speaker)
How many people watch the David Letterman Show?
Great! Then you will like our next comedian (or speaker).
He watches the show all the time, too!

* * * * * * *

(Pick money up off a table and put it in your pocket)
I really appreciate it when people tip the speaker! The
funny part is when I don't give it back!

(Someone's feet are on the stage)
Excuse me! Are you in show business?
No...then get your damn feet off the stage!

MICROPHONE

(If there's a short microphone cord)
My mom gave me more cord than this!

* * * * * * *

(When microphone feedback makes a screeching noise)
Quick impression, Jimi Hendrix!

* * * * * * *

(When the microphone stand collapses)
Has this ever happened to any of you guys before?

* * * * * * *

(When the microphone doesn't work)
I want to thank K-Mart for the sound system!

MISC.

(When no one responds to a question)
If you guys would play along, we will get out
of here a lot quicker!

* * * * * * *

(When you accidentally repeat yourself)
I just wanted to see if you guys were listening!

* * * * * * *

*(Often where you speak the drinks will be quite expensive
and an easy target to make fun of...)*
Enjoy the show and remember there's a 400 drink per
person minimum!

* * * * * * *

(You ask a question and get little response)
Wow! You can feel the energy in here!

* * * * * * *

How many people, by a show of hands,
are here for the first time...
(Pause for hands to raise)
and have never had sex?

(For a dead crowd)
I want to slow things down a little bit now!

RESTROOMS

(To someone returning from the restroom)
We had the video camera on in the restroom
while you were in there!
(Point to the curtains or wall)
Let's roll that film!

* * * * * * *

(When someone gets up to leave for the restroom)
No wait, I can be funnier!

* * * * * * *

*(When someone gets up to go to the restroom,
act as if you're controlling them)*
I'd like to ask one person to leave!

* * * * * * *

It's weird, every time I get up here people go
to the restroom!

* * * * * * *

(When someone gets up to leave for the restroom)
You can't get away from my jokes!
There's speakers in the restroom!

* * * * * * *

*(When someone goes to the restroom hide their chair and wait
for them to return)*
What's wrong?

SELF-PUT DOWNS

(You need to be able to take a joke as well as dish one out)

You're a great crowd! I'd like to end on a big laugh, but I don't see it happening here tonight!

* * * * * * *

If you want to see me on the Tonight Show, Thursday, February 23,...be sure to write and tell them!

* * * * * * *

I am going to go real slow now, because I only have one joke left!

* * * * * * *

Last night, the speaker before me was so bad, they were still booing him during MY act!

* * * * * * *

(When doing bad)
I want to thank you for helping me make a career decision tonight!

* * * * * * *

(After a bad show)
I've been up here almost an hour and I guess you guys win!

SELF-PUT DOWNS

(The audience will even enjoy watching you bomb if you have fun with it)
It's okay! My mom owns the club!

* * * * * * *

(When you're bombing)
It's okay! I've already been paid!

* * * * * * *

(Only one person laughs)
Could you run around the room, Sir, and make it sound like I'm doing well!

* * * * * * *

(When doing bad)
I don't need this job! I have a paper route!

* * * * * * *

(Look at watch)
I have to go now. I have another show to do...next year!

* * * * * * *

(When a joke gets a groan)
Come on! You'll all be telling that joke to your friends at the office tomorrow!

SELF-PUT DOWNS

Drink up! The more you drink, the funnier I get!

* * * * * * *

Whew! I was just in the back signing autographs! In fact, if you want one, they're still back there on the table!

* * * * * * *

I'm excited! I just signed a big record deal with Columbia Records! And my lawyer says the best thing about it is, I get the first twelve albums free!

* * * * * * *

Probably a lot of you people have problems and now you're staring at me saying,
"Boy, not even my life is that lousy!"

* * * * * * *

(If you screw up, avoid the embarrassment by putting yourself down)
Hey, F * * k me!

(When the audience laughs at their own response)
I hate it when the audience is funnier than I am!

STUPIDITY

What do you do for a living?
(When a person answers, "Nothing")
"Nothing," then how do you know when you're done?

* * * * * * *

Where are you from?
(When they only answer with the name of the state)
Can you be a little more vague?

* * * * * * *

Where are you from?
(When they just answer "Here")
I like the way you fixed the place up!
(Look around the restaurant, club, wherever you are)
These curtains (lights, etc.) are really nice!

* * * * * * *

(When someone doesn't respond to a question)
What happened, did you just go into a coma?

* * * * * * *

*(When someone doesn't answer you back, repeat the question
again real slow, and make gestures like you're asking the
question in sign language.)*

BONUS:

Patrick and Butch's Favorite Jokes

1) Three old men are in a rest home. One's seventy years old, one's eighty years old, and the third is ninety years old. They're sitting around talking one day and the seventy-year-old says, "I sure wish I could take a healthy piss again!" The eighty-year-old then says, "I can take a healthy piss, I just wish I could take a healthy crap again!" The ninety year old then responds, "Every morning around 9:30 A.M. I take a healthy piss, around 11:00 A.M. I take a healthy crap, I just wish I could wake up before noon!"

* * * * * * *

2) This father and mother have two sons, ten and eleven. The father and mother are sitting down at the breakfast table, eating breakfast, when the first son comes in, the eleven-year-old. He comes right up to the breakfast table, yanks out a chair, sits down, and says, "Give me some f * * kin' pancakes!" The father and mother can't believe their ears! The father gives his son the harshest lecture he's ever given him! He takes away his allowance, his bicycle, tells him no TV for a month, and sends him right up to his room! Just then he looks over at the doorway and sees his other son, the ten-year-old, standing there. The father goes, "And what do you want?" The son thinks for a minute and says, "Well, I'll tell you one thing, I sure don't want any of those f * * kin' pancakes!"

3) A teenage kid is working alone in an adult sex shop. A lady comes in and says, "I want a dildo." The kid says, "We have a white one for $50.00, and a black one for $100.00." The woman says, "I'll take the white one for $50.00!" She buys it and leaves. Another woman comes in and says, "I want a dildo." The kid says, "We have a black one for $100.00, and a white one for $50.00." The woman says, "I'll take the black one!" She leaves. A third woman comes in and says, "I want a dildo." The kid says, "We have a white one for $50.00, a black one for $100.00, and a plaid one for $350.00." The woman says, "Oh plaid sounds like fun!" She buys it and leaves. The manager comes back and says, "Hey kid, you sell anything?" He says, "Yes. I sold a white dildo for $50.00, a black dildo for $100.00, and my thermos for $350.00!"

* * * * * * *

4) A woman goes shopping for shoes with no panties on. She sits down and the salesman looks up her dress and says, "Damn baby, I'd like to fill that up with ice cream and eat it all up!" The woman is offended and says, "I'm going home to tell my husband!" She tells her husband, "Honey, I was shopping for shoes with no panties on, and the shoe salesman looked up my dress, and said he'd like to fill it all up with ice cream and eat it all up. Now what are you going to do about it?" The husband says, "There's three things I'll tell you. First of all, what are you doing shopping for shoes? There's a hundred pairs of shoes in your closet. You don't need any more shoes. Second, what are you doing shopping with no panties on, tell me that? And third of all, I'm not going to mess with no man who can eat that much ice cream!"

5) There's a farmer and his wife about to make love. They're naked facing each other. The farmer grabs his wife's breast and says, "You know honey, if these could give milk, we could get rid of the cows." The wife says, "That's right." The farmer grabs his wife's butt and says, "You know, if this could give eggs, we could get rid of the chickens." The wife says, "You're right." The wife then grabs her husband's dick and says, "You know, if this could stay hard, we could get rid of your brother!"

* * * * * * *

6) A manager is training a kid at K-Mart as a man walks up to the register with a bag of grass seed. The manager says, "Do you want a lawn mower to go along with that, Sir?" The man says, "What do I need a lawn mower for?" The manager says, "You're going to plant the grass, and it's going to grow, and then you'll need something to cut it with." The man thinks, then says, "Sure. I'll take the grass seed **and** the lawn mower," and then he leaves. The manager then says to the kid, "See how I did that? Next time when you're working alone and a customer comes up to the register with an item, sell him something to go along with it." Later that day the kid is working alone and a man comes up with a big box of Tampons and the kid says, "Do you want a lawn mower to go along with that, Sir?" The guy says, "What do I need a lawn mower for?" The kid says, "Well, your weekend is shot, you might as well cut the grass!"

7) A blind man walks into a department store with his dog and stops in the middle of it. He lifts his dog up by the tail and starts swinging it over his head. The manager runs up to him and says, "What do you think your doing?" The blind man replies, "Just looking around!"

* * * * * * *

8) A young boy wants a new bicycle and asks his mom. The mom tells her son to write a letter to God and ask him for $100.00 for a new bicycle. So the boy writes to God and asks him for $100.00 for his new bike. The postmaster gets the letter, reads it, and sends it to the President. The President reads the letter and writes the boy a letter on White House stationary with a check for $10.00 signed "God." The boy gets the letter, reads it, and tells his mother, "God sent me $10.00 to help me buy my bike." So the boy's mom tells her son to write a thank you note to God. So the boy writes a thank you note to God. The letter to God says, "Thank you for the $10.00 for my bike, but did you have to send the letter through Washington, the bums took 90%!"

9) There's a boy in the center of the street jumping up and down on a manhole cover, and he's saying, "Seventy-eight, seventy-eight!" An old man walks up and asks, "What are you doing?" The boy ignores him and keeps jumping up and down saying, "Seventy-eight, seventy-eight!" Finally, the man asks the kid if he can have a look. The boy lifts the manhole cover off and the man leans over to look in. Suddenly, the boy pushes the man in, puts the lid back on, and starts yelling, "Seventy-nine, seventy-nine!"

* * * * * * *

10) There's a bad accident, and the cops arrive. A couple has been killed, but there's a monkey that is still alive. The policeman says to the monkey, "Do you understand English?" The monkey nods, *Yes.* The policeman says, "Can you tell us what happened right before the accident occurred?" The monkey nods, *Yes.* The policeman says, "So what happened?" The monkey gestures, *Smoking pot.* The policeman says, "They were smoking pot?" The monkey nods *Yes.* "What else," asked the cop? The monkey gestures, *Drinking.* The cop says, "They were drinking booze?" The monkey nods *Yes.* The cop says, "What else?" The monkey gestures, *Sex.* The cop says, "They were having sex?" The monkey nods *Yes.* The cop says, "Okay, before the accident occurred, the couple was smoking pot, drinking booze, and having sex, is that right?" The monkey nods *Yes.* The cop says, "While all this was going on, monkey, what were you doing?" The monkey gestures, *Driving.*

11) There's a boy fishing and he has a pile of fish he's caught. A priest walks over and says, "What kind of fish are those?" The boy replies, "They're son-of-bitches fish." The Father says, "You shouldn't talk like that, little boy." The boy replies, "No Father, that's the name of the fishes, son-of-bitches." "Oh well, says the Father. "I'm going to have dinner with the Bishop tomorrow, can I have a couple to bring him?" The boy says, "Sure Father," and gives him some fish. The next day at dinner the fish are cooked and the priest tastes them and says, "My, these are great son-of-bitches fish!" The Bishop is stunned and says, "Father, you shouldn't talk like that!" The Father says, "No Bishop, that's the name of the fish, son-of-bitches fish." The Bishop says, "Oh well, they were great. Why don't we bring the leftover fish to the Pope's tomorrow for dinner." The next evening at dinner the fish are eaten by the Father and he says, "These are great son-of-bitches!" The Bishop says, "These sure are good son-of-bitches!" And the Pope stands up and says, "You know, you mother f * * kers are all right!"

* * * * * * *

12) A guy goes into a bar trying to meet a woman. He's there all night, but just can't seem to meet anyone. The next day he tells his roommate his problem. His roommate tells him when he goes into a bar, he should put a potato down his pants. So the next night the guy puts a potato down his pants and goes out. He stays at a club all night, but still doesn't meet any women. The following morning his roommate asks him how he did. He answers, "Terrible. I put the potato down my pants, spent all night in a bar, and didn't meet a single girl." The roommate thinks and says, "Next time try putting the potato down the *front* of your pants!"

13) There's a huge fire in this building and a lady's stuck on the twenty-second floor with her baby. The firemen arrive and the lady's screaming, "Save my baby, save my baby!" The firemen hold out this big net, but the lady won't toss her baby. So the fireman get Jerry Rice, the greatest football receiver of all time. The lady still doesn't want to toss her baby. The firemen yell up, "This is Jerry Rice, the greatest football receiver of all time. Lady, please toss your baby!" So the lady decides to toss her baby. The baby goes falling through the air and Jerry Rice runs left, then runs to the right, and then runs back to the left again and catches the baby! Jerry then says, "All right!" and spikes the baby into the ground!

The Driving Test

14) This is a fun party joke. On a piece of paper, draw a narrow, twisting road with lots of trees on the side. Then ask someone to take the driving test. Have them take their index finger, and starting at the bottom, drive all the way up the road to the end. Then have them drive all the way down the road. Have them do this several times until they think they have the road memorized. Next, have them do it with their eyes closed. As they're driving with their eyes closed, smack them on the forehead. When they ask why, tell them, "you hit a tree!"

Patrick Hanifin and **Butch Fisco** have been friends and stand-up comedians for 20 years. They have appeared on many national TV shows and performed at comedy clubs throughout the world.

Pretty women are encouraged to write.

TITLES BY CCC PUBLICATIONS

RETAIL $4.99

CAN SEX IMPROVE YOUR GOLF?
THE COMPLETE BOOGER BOOK
THINGS YOU CAN DO WITH A USELESS MAN
FLYING FUNNIES
MARITAL BLISS & OTHER OXYMORONS
THE VERY VERY SEXY ADULT DOT-TO-DOT BOOK
THE DEFINITIVE FART BOOK
THE COMPLETE WIMP'S GUIDE TO SEX
THE CAT OWNER'S SHAPE UP MANUAL
PMS CRAZED: TOUCH ME AND I'LL KILL YOU!
RETIRED: LET THE GAMES BEGIN
MALE BASHING: WOMEN'S FAVORITE PASTIME
THE OFFICE FROM HELL
FOOD & SEX
FITNESS FANATICS
YOUNGER MEN ARE BETTER THAN RETIN-A
BUT OSSIFER, IT'S NOT MY FAULT

RETAIL $4.95

1001 WAYS TO PROCRASTINATE
THE WORLD'S GREATEST PUT-DOWN LINES
HORMONES FROM HELL II
SHARING THE ROAD WITH IDIOTS
THE GREATEST ANSWERING MACHINE MESSAGES OF ALL TIME
WHAT DO WE DO NOW?? (A Guide For New Parents)
HOW TO TALK YOUR WAY OUT OF A TRAFFIC TICKET
THE BOTTOM HALF (How To Spot Incompetent Professionals)
LIFE'S MOST EMBARRASSING MOMENTS
HOW TO ENTERTAIN PEOPLE YOU HATE
YOUR GUIDE TO CORPORATE SURVIVAL
THE SUPERIOR PERSON'S GUIDE TO EVERYDAY IRRITATIONS
GIFTING RIGHT

RETAIL $5.95
50 WAYS TO HUSTLE YOUR FRIENDS ($5.99)
HORMONES FROM HELL
HUSBANDS FROM HELL
KILLER BRAS & Other Hazards Of The 50's
IT'S BETTER TO BE OVER THE HILL THAN UNDER IT
HOW TO REALLY PARTY!!!
WORK SUCKS
THE PEOPLE WATCHER'S FIELD GUIDE
THE UNOFFICIAL WOMEN'S DIVORCE GUIDE
THE ABSOLUTE LAST CHANCE DIET BOOK
FOR MEN ONLY (How To Survive Marriage)
THE UGLY TRUTH ABOUT MEN
NEVER A DULL CARD
RED HOT MONOGAMY (In Just 60 Seconds A Day) ($6.95)

RETAIL $3.95
YOU KNOW YOU'RE AN OLD FART WHEN...
NO HANG-UPS
NO HANG-UPS II
NO HANG-UPS III
GETTING EVEN WITH THE ANSWERING MACHINE
HOW TO SUCCEED IN SINGLES BARS
HOW TO GET EVEN WITH YOUR EXES
TOTALLY OUTRAGEOUS BUMPER-SNICKERS ($2.95)

NO HANG-UPS – CASSETTES   RETAIL $4.98
Vol. I: GENERAL MESSAGES (Female)
Vol. I: GENERAL MESSAGES (Male)
Vol. II: BUSINESS MESSAGES (Female)
Vol. II: BUSINESS MESSAGES (Male)
Vol. III: 'R' RATED MESSAGES (Female)
Vol. III: 'R' RATED MESSAGES (Male)
Vol. IV: SOUND EFFECTS ONLY
Vol. V: CELEBRI-TEASE